CW00855387

Creating Delicious Sausages

A detailed guide to making sausages.

By

J. D. Gilson

Copyright © 1998, 2001 by J. D. Gilson
All rights reserved.
No part of this book may be reproduced, stored in a retrieval system, or transmitted by any means, electronic, mechanical, photocopying, recording, or otherwise, without written permission from the author.

ISBN: 0-75961-993-X

This book is printed on acid free paper.

1stBooks - rev. 02/20/01

Table of Contents

Dedication

I wish to thank the many individuals who over the years guided me in developing this book.

One special thanks goes to my husband, who helped prepare many of the recipes.

Without their cooperation, this book would not have been possible.

INTRODUCTION

Making your own sausages will elevate your culinary standing among your family and friends. Having spent the last few years looking for sausage recipes, two factors became apparent to me. The vast variety of sausages and the lack of detailed recipes. To further complicate matters, every sausage maker has his or her own secret recipe for a particular kind of sausage.

Sausage making is almost a lost art. The smell of homemade plump, juicy sausages, cooking in your kitchen is an enjoyable experience. Making sausages is easy and fun. You will know exactly what ingredients are in the sausage and the conditions under which the sausage was prepared. The term sausage refers to dozens of different sausages, with great variation between types of sausages.

HISTORY OF SAUSAGES

In my research of sausage recipes, it became apparent that sausages differ as much from one country to another as the spices used in making them. There really is no such thing as "Italian sausage" or "Polish sausage" or any of the other dozens of ethnic sausages. What may be Italian or Polish sausage to one individual may not meet another individual's expectations of that particular sausage. A definition describing sausages is (A mixture of ground meats blended with herbs and spices).

Smoking and salting to preserve meat goes back to the time of the ancient Egyptians. Homer spoke enthusiastically of sausage in his Odyssey. The Roman's liking for sausage was so great; no festive occasion was considered complete without it. By the beginning of the Middle Ages sausages were common throughout Europe. People of the area that is now Germany, Poland, and Austria were making the same hearty wurst that we enjoy today.

Although sausage is usually made of pork, there is virtually no meat that can not be used. The process of sausage making evolved as an effort to economize and make use of whatever scraps of meat that were left over after an animal had been butchered.

In previous centuries the average diet of the lower class did not include meat on a daily basis. An example of this is from the book The Complete Sausage Book describing how sausages were used for special occasions; an example is Scandinavian Christmas sausage. When Christmas day arrived, the sausages were wrapped in gold foil and hung on the tree. Pigs were easy to raise and were valuable because they could eat scraps from the family table and root for food. Not only was the meat used in making sausage, but also the internal organs, the intestines for casings, the head cooked to remove all possible meat and made into a gel mixture. Sausages evolved out of necessity, but became an international element of food consumption.

Two factors are evident, the maximum utilization of all parts of the pig and the inventive flavorings developed by the ethnic groups throughout history. In preparing the variety of sausage recipes an understanding of ethnic groups evolved and an appreciation of the enormous food supply available today. Many sausages are made only in certain regions and are considered regional, where as ethnic sausages are more widely known. Regional sausages may no longer be made simply because of the lack of written recipes.

ABOUT SAUSAGES

All sausages fall into one of two groups, fresh or cured sausages. Fresh sausages must be cooked before eaten. These sausages must be treated like other fresh meat—kept cold when stored. Cured sausages are preserved with certain ingredients such as salt, nitrates or have been dried to prevent spoilage. Sodium nitrate or salt peter gives a red color to cured sausages after heating. Sausages, which do not contain a cure, will be brown after processing and will be less appealing.

Cures such as Morton Cure, Prague Powder, Intra Cure and Morton Tender Quick Mix can be purchased from grocery stores, or small commercial sausage makers. Follow directions on container. Cured sausages can be eaten as is or with only enough cooking to heat them through. Cures are used primarily to prevent botulism (food poisoning), to impart flavors and some preservation.

Prague Powder/Intra Cure No. 1 is a basic cure that is used to cure meats that require cooking, smoking and canning. The following directions for the use of Prague Powder No.1 are from the Great Sausages Recipe Book. It takes 4 oz. of Prague Powder No.1 to cure 100 lb. of sausage, 2 oz. for 50 lb. When curing 10 lb. of meat, it takes about ½ oz. of Prague Powder No.1. Put another way 4 level teaspoons equal about 1 oz of Prague Powder No.1 or 2 teaspoons will cure 10 lb. of sausage. Prague Powder/Intra Cure No. 2 is a cure formulated to be used with dry-cured products. Prague Powder No.2 can be compared to a time-released capsule. According to the Great Sausage Recipe Book sodium nitrate keeps breaking down into sodium nitrite, then nitric oxide, to cure the meat over extended periods of time. The amount of nitrite remaining in a cured product within two weeks after curing may be as little as one-fourth the initial amount.

FIVE KINDS OF SAUSAGES

Smoked Sausages ***(hot dogs, bologna) made from meat that has been cured and then smoked over wood fires.***

Cooked Sausages ***(liverwurst) made from meats that are either fresh or preserved by curing.***

Fresh Sausages ***(breakfast sausage or bratwurst) made from ground meats that have not been cooked or cured.***

Dry Sausages ***(dry salami) made from fresh meats that have been spiced, cured for several days, then dried for varying periods of time.***

Specialty Sausages ***made from unusual combinations of meats, grains, vegetables, and spices that are blended.***

HERBS AND SPICES

Spices and herbs are a small part of the complete mix, yet they play a very large part in the success of the recipe. Buy the best spices, date the container and throw out the unused spices after a year.

SALT

Salt is an important part of making good sausage. Salt is considered a spice because it enhances the favor of the sausage. According to the Great Sausage Recipe book a way to test for high grade salt is to dissolve one or two tablespoons in a glass of water, if the water is clear you have a good grade of salt. If the water is cloudy the salt may contain various heavy metals. Do not use iodized salt for making sausage. Canning or kosher salt is better since they dissolve completely. Salt acts as a binding agent.

FILLERS

The practice of extending sausages began as an economic measure, and is a good way of extending your meat dollars. Many commercial sausage makers use fat, but additional fat in your diet should be avoided. Wide ranges of fillers are used to extend meat and add favor: oatmeal, soybean, potato, and cabbage. A good rule to follow is not to use more than 1/3 filler ratio to your meat. More than 1/3 may change the taste and texture of your sausage.

SOY PROTEIN CONCENTRATE OR NON-FAT DRY MILK

The function non-fat milk or soy protein concentrates perform in sausage making is to bind the meat together and also to retain the natural juices of the meat. A rule to follow from the Great Sausage Recipe Book is do not use more than 5% soy protein concentrate or more than 12% non-fat dry milk, or you may alter the taste of the sausage.

HEALTHY SUBSTITUTES

If a recipe calls for an egg use two egg whites. Instead of salt use a salt substitute or omit salt entirely. Add other seasonings or have family member's salt at mealtime. Use turkey meat in place of pork, beef or veal. Use a combination of pork and turkey to reduce fat. If a recipe calls for two pounds of pork; use one pound pork and one pound of turkey meat. Add a filler such as oatmeal.

RULES FOR CLEANLINESS

Scrub all surfaces with soap and hot water that will come in contact with the meat. Assemble all your equipment and sterilize the utensils by pouring boiling water over them. Since modern grinders have plastic parts, boiling them for a period of time may damage the equipment. Remove your rings, watch, and wash your hands carefully.

CASINGS

Some types of casings are 1. natural or animal, 2. fibrous, 3. clothe, 4. cellulose. The nutritional value of natural casings is 80% collagen protein and 20% fat. The fat content is so small it is not included in the fat content of the sausage. Your local meat market/butcher shop can provide you with the casings you prefer. Sausage has to be stuffed into something, and most often the intestine of a hog, cow or sheep are used. The casings are cleaned and packed in salt, which keeps them fresh indefinitely. The natural casings come in an array of sizes, ranging from under one inch to over four inches. Sheep casings are similar in size to hot dogs and beef casings the size of a large salami. The hog casings are the most common since fresh sausages are made in two-inch diameter casings. All animal casings should be kept refrigerated or frozen until ready to use. If your butcher shop doesn't stock them, the butcher can order them for you.

PREPARING CASINGS

Snip off about four feet of casing. Rinse under cool water to remove salt. Soak in bowl over night. After soaking, slip one end of the casing over the faucet, turn on the cold water, gently rinse the inside of the casing out, increase water pressure flushing out the entire length of casing and remove any damaged portion of the casing. Place the cleaned casing in a bowl of water. Add one tablespoon of vinegar per cup of water this makes the casing more transparent and flexible. To minimize bacteria levels in natural and fibrous casings soak in vinegar or liquid smoke to prevent mold as recommended by the Great Sausage Recipes Book.

IF YOU DO NOT HAVE THE EQUIPMENT TO USE CASINGS, YOU CAN USE PLASTIC WRAP OR WAX PAPER.

Simply roll your sausage into lengths about 3 to 4 inches long and about 1 ½ to 2 inches thick. Wrap plastic or wax paper tightly around your sausage and refrigerate to firm up the sausage. Cook the sausage using a non-stick pan, fry gently as not to break up your sausage.

TOUGH CASINGS

To prevent tough casings rinse and flush casing, then refrigerate overnight. Flush the casing again before using. Do not put stuffed sausages in a hot smokehouse or smoker. The gradual raising of the temperature will prevent toughing of the casing. When preparing sausages never put sausages in boiling water. Start with cold water and bring the temperature up gradually to boil and then simmer until cooked.

MEAT CUTS FOR SAUSAGE MAKING

Most sausages are made from pork, beef, veal, and poultry or in various combinations. The most economical and efficient cuts of pork to use are from the neck, shoulder area, or rib end loin roast which have a good fat to lean ratio for making sausages. These are also suitable choices for veal. For beef the cheaper, fatter cuts, such as chuck, rump and shank cuts tend to be tastier. Occasionally lamb or poultry is called for in a recipe. Any kind of chicken or turkey will serve for the poultry. Lamb is a little tricky. Do not use lamb in combination with other meats, because the taste of lamb may overpower other meats. Whatever meat you buy, remember to allow for fat and bone. A four pound piece of pork with bone and fat will not yield four pounds of pork meat. **You may need five pounds to get the amount of meat you need.** A general rule for fat ratio for meat is ¼ fat to ¾ meat. General rule for venison is 1/3 fat to 2/3 meat or equal portions of ground pork and venison.

ONE CARDINAL RULE WHEN PURCHASING MEAT IS ALL MEAT FOR SAUSAGE MUST BE FRESHLY GROUND.

FAT

Most recipes call for a certain amount of fat. You can minimize the amount of fat you put in your sausage, but do not eliminate fat completely. The fat serves several purposes adding flavor, helping bind the mixture of meat, and lubricating the casings.

EQUIPMENT

Have everything together and in its place before you start any recipe. Devices for making sausage range from the simple to the complex and from dirt cheap to outrageously expensive. The old fashion grinders like grandmother had are still available. There are a wide variety of electrical grinders available. Whichever type of food grinder you purchase, choose one that has two or more cutting disks for coarse and fine jobs. Some electric food grinders come with a sausage funnel or you can purchase a sausage funnel from a butcher supply store, restaurant supply store or it can be ordered through the mail. If your grinder doesn't have a sausage stuffing attachment, an alternative is to use plastic wrap or wax paper. This technique was discussed in the casing section. A homemade sausage stuffer for larger casings can be made from a piece of plastic or stainless steel pipe and a wooden dowel sawed off to fit inside the plastic or steel pipe. The following is a guide to grinding different textures of meat: coarse grind = 3/8 plate, medium grind = 3/16 plate, fine grind = 3/8 inch plate followed by 1/8 inch plate.

When not working with meat keep refrigerated.

If you did not purchased your meat already ground, cut the meat into one-inch cubes. Refrigerate the meat for about ½ to 1 hour to firm up before grinding. Put meat through grinder using coarse disk. Follow the directions of your recipe for remaining ingredients. Mix well; grind meat mixture again if you want a finer texture. At this point, refrigerate the meat for an hour, it will be easier to handle when stuffing. Rub oil on the sausage funnel, this will allow the casing to slide on easier. Push it along until it is all on the funnel; pull just enough casing off to tie a knot at the end.

Begin stuffing the casing with meat mixture. Watch for air bubbles, holes or breaks in the casing. If air bubbles develop, sterilize the end of a needle and puncture air bubbles. Do not be afraid of loosing juices, the hole will re-seal when cooked. If the casing should break or tear while you are stuffing, tie off the sausage at that point and continue stuffing the undamaged portion. Stop stuffing when each link is just a little less thicker than you want it to be. The meat mixture contained within will expand as you cook the sausage and may burst if over stuffed. Force the meat through the funnel, stuffing the casing, maintaining an even flow to avoid air pockets. Beginning at the tied end of the casing, grasp about four inches of sausage and twist two or three times in the same direction. Grasp another four inches of sausage and twist in the opposite direction. Refrigerate sausage for 1 to 2 hours, this helps prevent sausage from untwisting. With a sharp knife (not serrated knife-since this type tends to tear the casing) cut the links apart. Some sausages are cooked and eaten immediately after stuffing, while others require special procedures such as smoking and drying.

SMOKING

The process of smoking meat originated many centuries ago when few other means of preserving meat were available. Smoking helps dry sausages quickly, lessening their susceptibility to decay. The chemicals in the smoke impart flavor, aroma, improve the appearance and texture of some sausages.

HINTS WHEN SMOKING

One important factor to remember is the smoke must be kept moving freely around the meat, but still be somewhat confined. Do not enclose your meat tightly, too much smoke can be unpalatable. A slow burning wood fire is an ideal source of fuel. You may use charcoal sprinkled with a fine layer of sawdust. Fruit woods (apple, cherry, pear trees are good sources of wood) hickory, oak and maple wood.

Never use softwood such as pine, cedar, spruce, hemlock, fir or cypress.

Soft wood gives off a sooty smoke and your sausage will be a dark color and have a bitter taste. Be sure the wood is not dry or your fire will be to hot (soak wood for 20 minutes in water). Smoke only meat that is dry on the surface. A wet surface prevents meat from gaining a uniform color. Light the fire. Wait 30 to 40 minutes, when flames have died down, hang your sausages or place on rack.

Be sure sausages Do Not touch one another or the sides of the smoker.

The entire surface of the meat must be exposed to ensure an even color.

It is simple to create food poisoning, a temperature of 40-140 degrees F., moisture, and lack of oxygen are key elements. The internal temperature of the sausage must be at less 160 degrees F. There are some exceptions when making sausage with meat other than pork, but when in doubt be safe at 160 degrees F.

Hang a thermometer on a rack/bar. Follow directions for smoking in each recipe. (You may wish to increase or decrease the time depending on your taste in sausage). Add slightly damp wood to the smoker as needed.

Keep a log in which you record smoking times and any additional methods. You can repeat the process if you hit upon a magic formula for a particular flavor.

Purchase a smoker and follow the manufacture's directions.

LIQUID SMOKE

To obtain good distribution in fine or coarse chopped sausage, dilute the liquid smoke with the water you will use in the recipe or if not using water than in ¼ cup of water. 4 oz. for 100 pounds of meat and 1 teaspoon for 5 pounds of meat. If you do not want to purchase a smoker follow these rules. Add 1 teaspoon of liquid smoke for every 5 pounds of meat. Place in oven at 160 to 165 degrees on a rack in a shallow pan. Add 1 cup of water to pan for moisture. Keep oven door open slightly. Turn meat occasionally, approximate time of cooking 5 to 7 hours and the internal sausage temperature should reach 160 degree F. or as specified in recipe.

SHOWERING WITH COLD WATER

Showering the sausage with cold water is to prevent the sausage from shriveling up. This happens quickly, the sausage should be put under cold water promptly after removal from the smoker. If the sausage should become shriveled put it into hot water and cook to bring back its firmness, then shower with cold water immediately.

DRYING

An excellent idea was found in the Home Sausage Cookbook for the drying process that follows. If you have a second refrigerator remove all the shelves except the top one. From this shelf you can tie the links of sausage and let them hang. **DO NOT LET THEM TOUCH ONE ANOTHER.** If you can not devote this much space to the sausage, place on a shelf and turn frequently to promote even drying. The temperature must be adjusted to remain fairly constant 38 to 40 deg. F. If the refrigerator has a fan, adjust so as not to blow constantly. A constant stream of air would cause the sausage to dry on the outside before the inside has a chance to mature. According, to the Great Sausage Recipe Book a moisture removal of 25% is considered a fully dried product when done at 30 to 40 deg. F. When curing dry sausages, the sausage should be spaced as not to touch each other. The length of time the sausage is dried cured depends on the diameter of the sausage. For further information refer to “Government Regulations for Curing Dry or Semi-Dry Sausages”.

SWEETENERS/CORN SYRUP SOLIDS

Powdered dextrose can be used as a browning agent. Powdered dextrose is about 70% as sweet as granulated sugar and heavier, forcing itself into the cells of the meat. Powdered dextrose is used in the processing of dry-cured or semi-dry cured sausages. It assists in fermentation and gives the desired flavor. Another example of a sweetener is maple syrup giving sausage a distinctive flavor. Corn syrup solids provide excellent binding qualities when sausage is cured at lower temperatures and helps retain the color of the sausage. Corn syrup also helps support the fermentation process.

Cooking Sausages

It is important that minced meats such as sausages are thoroughly cooked. The germs causing food poisoning can be all the way through the meat, not just on the outside surface. If the meat is pink inside or any juices are pink rather than clear, the meat is undercooked.

Defrosting Meat

Allow meat to partially defrost slowly in the refrigerator or partially defrost in a microwave. Partially frozen meat is easier to grind.

FRESH SAUSAGES

The recipes have been reduced to smaller quantities for you to try and then double or triple the recipes that you prefer. Where possible the source of the original recipe has been noted at the end of the recipe.

Basic Pork Sausage – Version 1

1 pound ground pork

1/8 teaspoon red pepper

¼ teaspoon salt

½ teaspoon black pepper

½ teaspoon crushed sage

Mix all ingredients and form into patties or stuff into casings.

Pork Sausage – Version 2

3 pounds ground pork

2 ½ teaspoons dried marjoram

2 ½ teaspoons salt

½ teaspoon garlic powder

¼ to ½ teaspoon pepper

1 cup milk

1 medium onion, diced fine

¼ teaspoon paprika

¼ teaspoon sage

2 slices of bread

1 egg

Soak bread in milk for 5 minutes and mix all ingredients together. Form into patties or stuff into casings for links. For a variation use tomato juice in place of the milk. (Healthier Sausages)

Spicy Breakfast Sausage

1 pound ground pork

1/8 cup chopped onion

1/8 teaspoon garlic powder

1 teaspoon chopped parsley

1/8 teaspoon marjoram

1/8 teaspoon cayenne pepper

1/8 teaspoon thyme

1/8 teaspoon basil

½ teaspoon pepper

½ teaspoon salt

Mix all ingredients together. Form into patties or stuff into casings (Healthier Sausages)

Onion Sausage

1 pound pork butt

2 teaspoons salt

1/4 cup finely chopped onion

1 teaspoon black course pepper

1 teaspoon ground marjoram

1/4 cup ice water

Grind pork butt with coarse grinder plate, then add all remaining ingredients, mixing until evenly distributed. Stuff sausage into casings and refrigerate for 24 hours before using. (Great Sausage Recipe Book)

Veal Sausages

1 pound veal

1/4 pound smoked bacon

1/2 teaspoon sage

1/2 teaspoon salt

1 teaspoon black pepper

1 teaspoon parsley

Grind veal and bacon. Add seasonings, mix together and form into patties. (Great Sausage Recipe Book)

Cabbage Pork Sausages

1 ½ pounds boneless pork butt

½ teaspoon ground white pepper

1 teaspoon sage

1/8 teaspoon ground ginger

½ teaspoon ground nutmeg

½ teaspoon thyme

1 teaspoon ground hot red pepper

1 tablespoon salt

1 teaspoon sugar

½ chopped onion

1 pound cabbage (core removed)

Quarter cabbage and boil in water until tender. Remove cabbage, drain and cool. Grind cabbage through a (coarse = 3/16 inch grinder plate) along with onions and meat. Add remaining ingredients and mix well, stuff into casings. Refrigerate or freeze.

(The Complete Sausage Cookbook)

Sausage Cakes

1 pound pork

4 slices country smoked bacon

½ teaspoon salt

1 teaspoon black pepper

1 teaspoon parsley

¼ teaspoon nutmeg

¼ cup chopped onion

6 to 8 saltine crackers

Grind meat, use saltine crackers to clean out grinder, mix seasonings and form into patties. Flour patties and fry. (The Complete Sausage Cookbook)

Sausage Meat

1 pound ground pork

¼ pound ground round steak

2 to 3 crushed saltine crackers

1 tablespoon sugar

1 teaspoon salt

1 teaspoon black pepper

1 teaspoon summer savory

1 teaspoon sage

Mix all ingredients together, form into patties or stuff into links. (The Complete Sausage Cookbook)

SAUSAGES FROM AROUND THE WORLD

Bockwurst-Austria

2-3 feet casings

1 ½ pounds veal

½ pound side pork

¼ cup finely chopped onion

1 cup cream

1 egg

¾ teaspoon ground cloves

½ teaspoon ground white pepper

1 teaspoon finely chopped parsley

1 teaspoon salt

1 teaspoon nutmeg

½ teaspoon mace

Prepare the casings, grind veal and side pork until fine. Add remaining ingredients and mix well. Stuff into casings and twist off into 3 or 4 inch links. The sausage may be refrigerated or frozen, to eat immediately simmer for thirty minutes and then brown. (Home Sausage Making)

Vienna Sausage-Austria

3 feet casing

1 ½ pounds ground pork

2 tablespoons diced onion

1 teaspoon sugar

½ teaspoon cayenne red pepper

1 teaspoon paprika

½ teaspoon finely ground mace

1 ½ teaspoons salt

1/3 cup flour

½ cup water

Prepare casings, grind meat and mix with remaining ingredients. Stuff into casings or make patties.

Belgian Trippe-Belguim

2 ½ pounds ground pork

1 pound ground beef

1 medium onion, chopped fine

16 cups cut up raw cabbage

1 teaspoon sage

1 teaspoon nutmeg

1 teaspoon marjoram

3 tablespoons salt

2 teaspoons pepper

Boil cabbage, cool, squeeze out water. Mix all ingredients, put through grinder to grind cabbage and put in casings. Brown sausages in pan when ready to serve.

Belgian Summer Sausage

2 pounds ground beef

¼ teaspoon onion powder

1 teaspoon mustard seed

½ teaspoon garlic powder

1 teaspoon Morton Tender-Quick Salt

½ teaspoon black pepper

1 teaspoon liquid smoke

1 cup water.

Mix all ingredients well, make two rolls, wrap in plastic wrap and refrigerate over night. Bake on a rack in a 300 degree oven until internal temperature of the sausage is 160 degrees. Put a pan on bottom rack to catch drippings. (St. Joseph's Church Cookbook)

Kebabce, Veal or Lamb Sausage-Bulgaria

1 pound veal or lamb

½ onion minced

½ teaspoon salt

½ teaspoon pepper

½ teaspoon nutmeg

1 egg

Mix meat and remaining ingredients, put in refrigerator for 1 hour to set. Take small portions (about 1-tablespoon) form in round balls, then into 2 inch sausages. These are best cooked over charcoal heat but can be fried. Can serve hot or cold as hors d'oeuvres.

(The Complete Sausage Cookbook)

Cantonese Sausage-China

1 ¼ pounds ground pork

1 ½ teaspoons salt

1/8 cup honey

2 tablespoons orange juice

2 teaspoons white vinegar

¼ cup soy sauce

¼ cup rice wine

Combine all ingredients, mix well, and stuff into casings. Cook in peanut oil.

(The Complete Sausage Cookbook)

Cuban Sausage

1 pound lean sausage

¼ pound side pork

1 ½ teaspoons salt

½ teaspoon pepper

1 garlic clove, crushed

¼ teaspoon cumin

½ teaspoon oregano

1/8 cup paprika

¼ cup water

Grind meat, add remaining ingredients and mix well. Stuff into casings, dry in refrigerator for 6 hours before using. (The Complete Sausage Cookbook)

Leverpolse-Liver Sausage Denmark

¾ pound liver

½ pound fresh pork

1½ teaspoons grated onion

½ teaspoon salt

¼ teaspoon black pepper

¼ teaspoon allspice

¼ teaspoon thyme

Grind meat fine, add remaining ingredients, and mix well. Stuff into casings and boil for 20 minutes.

(The Complete Sausage Cookbook)

Medisterrolse-Pork Sausage Denmark

2 pounds pork

½ pound side pork

½ cup onion grated

½ cup stock beef or chicken

½ teaspoon black pepper

1½ teaspoons salt

¼ teaspoon allspice

¼ teaspoon ground cloves.

Grind meat fine, add remaining ingredients and stuff into casings, not too firmly.

(The Complete Sausage Cookbook)

Yorkshire Polony England

3 ¾ pounds lean pork

1 ½ pounds side pork

8 oz rice flour

8 oz fine white rusk

2 ½ tablespoons salt and 1 ¼ teaspoons pepper

1 tablespoon mace

1 ½ teaspoons coriander

1 ½ teaspoons nutmeg

¾ teaspoon cinnamon

Grind meat finely, mix remaining ingredients, fill wide hog casings and tie into rings. Cook for 25 minutes, and then plunge into a salt solution to fix color. A good salt solution will allow a raw egg to float.

(The Complete Sausage Cookbook)

Riisimakkara-Rice and Liver Sausage Finland

½ pound liver, sliced

1 medium onion minced

½ cup butter

2 cups cooked rice, chilled

2 eggs, slightly beaten

½ cup milk

1 cup raisins (optional)

¼ cup dark corn syrup

¼ teaspoon ginger

½ teaspoon white pepper

3 teaspoons salt

Grind meat fine, brown liver and onion until the red color disappears. Turn into mixing bowl and add remaining ingredients. The mixture will be thin. Stuff into casings loosely, approximately 6 inch links. Put into large pot in one layer and add water to cover. Simmer for 30 minutes, occasionally pricking the sausage. Drain and cool. To serve, bake or brown sausage in butter until heated through. (The Complete Sausage Cookbook)

Boudin Blanc-French Sausage

1 pound veal

1 pound chicken breast

½ pound side pork

1 cup milk

¾ cup bread crumbs

¼ teaspoon nutmeg

¼ teaspoon allspice

¼ teaspoon white pepper

2 teaspoons salt

1 tablespoon parsley, chopped

1 tablespoon chives, chopped

4 eggs

1 cup half and half

Boudin Blanc-French Sausage - continued

Prepare casing; grind the side pork, chicken and veal with fine disk. Chop onion and soak breadcrumbs in milk. Combine all remaining ingredients and grind once more if desired. Stuff into casings. To cook cover sausages with a mixture of ½ milk and ½ water, simmer for about ½ hour or until done. (Home Sausage Making)

Bratwurst-Origin Nuremberg, Germany

3 feet of casing

2 pounds ground pork

1 pound ground veal

¼ teaspoon ground allspice

½ teaspoon caraway seed

½ teaspoon dried marjoram

¾ teaspoon white pepper

1 ½ teaspoons salt

1 medium finely chopped onion

Prepare the casing. Mix ground meats and onion. Add the remaining ingredients to the meat mixture and mix thoroughly. Stuff the mixture into casings and twist off into 4 or 5-inch links. Bratwurst can be pan fried or grilled. (Home Sausage Making)

German Bratwurst

1 pound coarse ground pork

1 pound ground veal

2 teaspoons celery seed

2 teaspoons caraway seed

2 tablespoons dry milk

1 egg

2 teaspoons onion powder

½ teaspoon salt and pepper and small amount of grated lemon peel.

1 teaspoon dried parsley

3 tablespoons water

Combine all ingredients and mix well. Let stand 1 hour and mix again. Stuff into casings or fry as patties. (The Complete Sausage Cookbook)

Knockwurst Germany

1 pound beef

1 pound pork

½ pound side pork

1 teaspoon garlic powder

¼ cup finely chopped onion

1 ½ teaspoons coriander

½ teaspoon mace

1 teaspoon salt

½ cup water

Cube, grind meats and add remaining ingredients. Stuff into casing forming 5-6 inch links and tie off securely. Place sausage in a large kettle, cover with water, bring to boil and simmer for 15 minutes. Drain and rinse with cold water, when cool hand dry. Refrigerate or freeze. (Home Sausage Making)

Frankfurters/Hot Dogs

1 ½ pounds pork

½ pound beef

½ pound side pork

¼ cup chopped onion

½ teaspoon garlic powder

1 teaspoon ground coriander

1/8 teaspoon marjoram

¼ teaspoon ground mace

¼ teaspoon mustard seed

1 teaspoon paprika

1 teaspoon white pepper

1 egg white

1 teaspoon sugar

1 teaspoon salt

½ cup water

Frankfurters/Hot Dogs - continued

Prepare the casings, grind the meats, and add remaining ingredients. Chill mixture for ½ hour. Stuff into casings and twist off into 6-inch links. Parboil the links (without separating them—tie off each open end) simmer in water for 20 minutes. Place the franks in a bowl of ice water, chill. Remove, pat dry and refrigerate or freeze.

(Home Sausage Making)

Greek Orange Sausage

1 ½ pounds ground pork

1 pound ground beef

1 ½ cloves garlic, crushed

1/8 cup orange rind, chopped

1 ½ teaspoons cinnamon

1 ½ teaspoons allspice

1½ teaspoons black pepper

1½ teaspoons salt

½ cup white wine

Peel orange removing only the peel and not the white part. Put peel, garlic, cinnamon, allspice, pepper, salt and wine in blender, and blend until orange peel is finely chopped. Mix well into meat and stuff into casings or form patties. (The Complete Sausage Cookbook)

Haitian Sausage

1 pound raw shrimp, shelled and cleaned

½ pound boiled ham

2 pounds lean beef

1 cup minced onions

3 large garlic cloves, crushed

2 tablespoons hot red pepper flakes

½ teaspoon cayenne

1 tablespoon each of salt and pepper

2 cups dry breadcrumbs

2 medium onions sliced-use only one in meat mixture

2 medium sized bay leaves-use in water bath.

2 eggs

Chop shrimp and ham-set aside. Grind beef, add shrimp, ham, onion, garlic, pepper flakes, cayenne, salt, black pepper and mix well. Beat eggs, add ½ cup of breadcrumbs to the beaten eggs with 1-tablespoon water, and pour into pan. Roll sausages first in egg mixture then in breadcrumbs.

Haitian Sausage - continued

Wrap sausage in unbleached muslin clothes and secure. Bring salt water to boil, add sliced onions, bay leaves and simmer for one hour. Remove sausage and cool.

(The Complete Sausage Cookbook/Riddle/Danley)

Hazi Kolbasz-Hungary

2 ½ pounds ground pork

2 cloves garlic

1 tablespoon salt

1 tablespoon black pepper

2 teaspoons paprika

¼ teaspoon ground cloves

½ lemon rind, grated

½ cup water

Combine all ingredients and stuff into casings. To serve bake for 1 hour at 350 degrees F.

(The Complete Sausage Cookbook)

Hungarian Sausage

1 pound ground pork

½ pound ground beef

4 strips of side pork

½ cup of water

1 teaspoon garlic powder

2 teaspoons salt

½ teaspoon pepper

1 tablespoon paprika

1/8 teaspoon ground cloves

Grind all meats. Add remaining ingredients and mix well. Form into patties or make into links.

(Home Sausage Making)

Irish Sausage

2 ½ pounds ground pork

2 ½ cups bread crumbs

2 eggs, lightly beaten

4 cloves garlic, crushed

1 ½ teaspoons salt

1 ½ teaspoons thyme

1 ½ teaspoons basil

1 ½ teaspoons rosemary

1 ½ teaspoons marjoram

1 ½ teaspoons black pepper

1 cup water

Combine all ingredients, mix well, and stuff into casings. Fry in butter or oil.

(The Complete Sausage Cookbook)

Israel

Passover Sausages

1 pound chopped beef

¼ cup onion, grated

1 small carrot

1 egg, beaten

2 tablespoons cold water

Fine matzo meal

Combine meat, onion, beaten egg with water and salt if desired. Grate in carrot, and mix well. Form ½ inch-thick sausage links about 2 ½ inches long. Roll in matzo meal, and fry until browned on all sides. Drain excess fat on paper towel. Makes about 24 sausages.
(The Complete Sausage Cookbook)

Kosher Bratwurst

Substitute equalivant amounts of beef and veal for pork and follow directions for bratwurst recipe. Example: 2 pounds pork use 2 pounds beef and the amount of veal required.

Israeli Salami

2 ½ pounds ground beef

¾ pound beef fat

1 ½ teaspoons crushed coriander

2 tablespoons salt

1 ½ tablespoons sugar

1 ½ teaspoons black pepper

½ cup white wine

1 ½ teaspoons paprika

1 teaspoon ground ginger

½ teaspoon nutmeg

4 cloves garlic, crushed

1 teaspoon quick tender salt or saltpeter

Grind meats fine. Combine all ingredients and mix well. Refrigerate for 48 hours, then stuff into fiber or cellulose casings. Smoke for 6 to 8 hours, slowly increasing the temperature to 160 degrees until the internal temperature of the sausage is 160 degrees. Chill the sausage in cold water, and dry for 3 weeks.

(The Complete Sausage Cookbook)

Meatless Hot Dogs

1 pound chickpeas (garbanzo beans)

1 cup soft bread crumbs

2 eggs, slightly beaten

1 teaspoon garlic

1 teaspoon salt

½ teaspoon pepper

1 teaspoon cumin seed

1 teaspoon cayenne

1/4 teaspoon hot red pepper flakes

½ teaspoon baking powder

Rinse the chickpeas well and soak for 8 hours or overnight. Grind the chickpeas through a course plate. Add remaining ingredients, mix well. Stuff into fiber casings and refrigerate.

(The Complete Sausage Cookbook/Riddle/Danley)

Mild Italian Sausage

2 pounds ground pork

2 teaspoons paprika

1 teaspoon garlic powder

1 ½ teaspoons fennel seed

1 teaspoon black pepper

¼ teaspoon crushed red pepper

½ teaspoon salt

Mix all ingredients, and form into patties, stuff into casings or fry loose for pizza. (Healthier Sausages)

Hot Italian Sausage

2 pounds ground pork

1/3 medium onion chopped fine

1 teaspoon garlic powder

1 teaspoon salt

1 teaspoon pepper

1 teaspoon paprika

1 teaspoon crushed red pepper

1 teaspoon fennel seed

1/8 teaspoon thyme

¼ cup of water

Mix all ingredients, form into patties, stuff into casings or fry loose for pizza. Variation: add ½ to 1 cup of grated Parmesan cheese. (Healthier Sausages)

Pork and Shiitake Mushroom Sausage – Japan

1 pound pork shoulder

½ pound side pork

½ pound chicken or turkey meat

6 oz. dried Shiitake mushrooms

2 tablespoons soy sauce

1/8 cup sweet sherry

½ teaspoon grated lime zest

½ teaspoon ginger

½ teaspoon sugar

1 ½ teaspoons sesame oil

1 tablespoon rice vinegar

Soak mushrooms in hot water for 30 minutes. Remove and discard stems, drain and chop fine. Grind pork, poultry and side pork. Add remaining ingredients and mix well. Stuff into casings or leave bulk.

(The Complete Sausage Cookbook)

Lithuanian Sausage

2 pounds ground pork

1/3 pound smoked ham

¼ cup chopped onion

½ teaspoon garlic powder

1 tablespoon of butter

2 teaspoons black pepper

½ teaspoon white pepper

½ teaspoon allspice

Grind meats, sauté onions and garlic in butter until limp. Cool and add to meat along with seasonings. Stuff into casings at 4 to 5 inch lengths. Add ½ cup salt to 2 quarts of water, place links in solution and refrigerate overnight. Drain and pat dry with paper towel. Use within 2 or 3 days or freeze.

(The Complete Sausage Cookbook/Riddle/Danley)

Mexican Chorizo Sausage

2 pounds ground pork

¼ pound side pork

5 to 6 dried chili peppers

½ cup red wine vinegar

½ medium onion, quartered

2 to 4 garlic cloves, minced

2 ½ teaspoons salt

2 teaspoons oregano

½ teaspoon cumin

½ teaspoon cayenne

Soak chilies in vinegar until soft. Remove stems, place chilies and vinegar into blender with quartered onion and puree. Grind meats, add remaining ingredients, and mix well. Refrigerate at least 2 hours or overnight. Shape into patties or links. (The Complete Sausage Cookbook)

Moroccan Lamb Sausage

1 ½ pounds lamb

½ cup chopped parsley

½ cup minced onion

½ teaspoon marjoram

1/8 teaspoon cumin

½ teaspoon coriander

½ teaspoon oregano

½ teaspoon cayenne

½ teaspoon black pepper

½ teaspoon salt

Cube the lamb meat and grind coarsely. Add remaining ingredients and mix well. Grind again. Stuff into casings or make patties.

(The Complete Sausage Cookbook/Riddle/Danley)

Norway

Sorlands-Kumper-Raw Potato Sausage

1 pound ground pork

6 raw potatoes

1 cup oatmeal

1 tablespoon salt

1 teaspoon thyme

1 cup flour

½ cup sugar

½ teaspoon white pepper

½ teaspoon ginger

½ package seedless raisins

Mix well, and fill in sausage shaped muslin bags, which have first been dipped in cold water. Drop sausages into boiling salt water; boil slowly for 1-½ hours.

(The Complete Sausage Cookbook)

Norwegian Sausage

1 ¼ pounds ground beef

¾ pound ground pork

¾ teaspoon salt

½ medium onion grated

1 ¼ teaspoons nutmeg

Mix all ingredients, stuff into casings. Simmer in one can chicken broth and sufficient water to cover sausages for ½ hour. Drain, cool, freeze or store in refrigerator and use within two days. (Healthier Sausages)

Puerto Rican Turkey and Ham Sausage

4 pounds turkey meat

½ pound boiled ham

5 eggs

½ pound fresh mushrooms sliced

1 ½ teaspoons salt

½ teaspoon nutmeg

½ teaspoon cayenne

½ teaspoon dry mustard

½ teaspoon black pepper

1 cup seasoned breadcrumbs

Mix turkey with ham, grind together, add 4 of the eggs, one at a time, and beat each one in well. Add mushrooms, salt, nutmeg, cayenne, dry mustard and pepper. Blend well; add enough breadcrumbs for mixture to hold together when shaped. Shape into two sausages 8 to 10 inches long and 2 to 3 inches thick. Roll the sausage first in the remaining beaten egg and then in bread crumbs, making sure both ends are covered. Case in 3 layers of cheesecloth. Put in boiling stock and simmer for 1 hour. Remove from stock and refrigerate for 24 hours before using. (The Complete Sausage Cookbook)

Fresh Polish Sausage

1 pound pork

1 teaspoon dried marjoram

½ teaspoon salt

¼ teaspoon garlic powder

½ teaspoon black pepper

1/8 teaspoon poultry seasoning

1/8 teaspoon sage

¼ cup water

Grind meat. Mix all ingredients thoroughly and form into patties or stuff into casings. (Healthier Sausages)

Spicy Fresh Polish Kielbasa-also referred to as Polish Sausage

3 feet of casing

1 ½ pounds pork butt cubed

½ pound beef chuck cubed

1 ½ teaspoons salt

1 ½ teaspoons black pepper

½ teaspoon marjoram

½ teaspoon savory

1/8 teaspoon allspice

½ teaspoon garlic powder

1 tablespoon paprika

Prepare the casings/grind the meats. Mix remaining ingredients with meat. Stuff into casing 18 inches long. Refrigerate sausage uncovered for 24 hours to dry. Cook by roasting in a 425 degree F. oven for 45 minutes with a small amount of water in pan. (Healthier Sausages)

Polish Blood Sausage

2 cups water

2 ½ pounds pork butt

½ cup pearl barley or rice

½ pound side pork

2 quarts pig blood

2 teaspoons vinegar add to blood (stops coagulation)

½ teaspoon ginger

1 teaspoon allspice

1 teaspoon black pepper

1 tablespoon salt

1 clove garlic, crushed

2 teaspoons baking soda

½ cup minced onion

Flour

Polish Blood Sausage - continued

Boil water; add barley or rice cover and simmer for 15 minutes. Drain and cool. Grind meats; add remaining ingredients except baking soda. Add enough flour to thicken the batter consistency, add baking soda. May be stuffed into hog casings or processed by the following method: Make casings from strong closely woven muslin. Fill sacks ¾ full, tie ends tightly. Place in boiling salted water simmering for 1 ½ to 2 hours over medium heat. Remove, drain and cool.

Linguica-Portuguese Sausage

2 pounds pork

1 ¼ teaspoons salt

2 to 4 garlic cloves, minced

2 to 3 dried hot chili peppers, crushed

1 ½ teaspoons coriander

1 ½ teaspoons paprika

¼ teaspoon cinnamon

¼ teaspoon ground cloves

¼ teaspoon allspice

1/8 cup cider vinegar

¼ cup cold water

Grind meat coarsely, combine with remaining ingredients and mix well. Cover and chill for at least two hours or overnight. Shape into patties or links.

(The Complete Sausage Cookbook)

Metitie Romanian Sausage

2 pounds ground beef

¼ teaspoon garlic powder

1 teaspoon baking soda

½ teaspoon allspice

½ teaspoon thyme

1 teaspoon salt and 1 teaspoon pepper

½ cup beef stock

1/3 cup chopped parsley

Cube meat, grind twice, and mix together ingredients. With moist hands form sausages about 3 inches long and about ¾ inch thick. Brush sausages with oil, grill or broil turning until nicely brown. (Home Sausage Making)

Romanian Beef Sausage

2 ½ pounds ground beef chuck

2 ½ teaspoons salt

½ teaspoon black pepper

3 garlic cloves, crushed

½ teaspoon baking soda

½ teaspoon crushed cloves

1 tablespoon sugar

Combine all ingredients, mix well and stuff into casings. (The Complete Sausage Cookbook)

Russian Sausage

2 ½ pounds ground pork

1 large onion, chopped

1 tablespoon pressed garlic

½ cup fresh parsley, chopped

1 ½ tablespoons dill seed

1 ½ tablespoons caraway seed

1 ½ teaspoons black pepper

1 ½ teaspoons salt

1 cup of water

Combine all ingredients, and mix well. Stuff into hog casings. To prepare bake for 1 hour.

(The Complete Sausage Cookbook)

Chorizos- Spain

2 ½ pounds pork

2 cloves garlic, minced

¾ cup onion, chopped

2 teaspoons salt

¾ teaspoon freshly ground black pepper

2 teaspoons Spanish paprika

½ teaspoon dried ground chili peppers

1 teaspoon cumin

Grind meat, add all ingredients and mix well. Fill casings or form into patties. When ready to use, cook over very low heat until cooked through.

(The Complete Sausage Cookbook)

Hot Spanish Sausage

1 pound ground pork

1/8 cup vinegar

½ teaspoon oregano

1 teaspoon garlic powder

½ teaspoon chili powder

½ teaspoon pepper

½ teaspoon salt

¼ teaspoon ground cumin

½ teaspoon crushed red pepper

½ teaspoon (cayenne) pepper

Mix all ingredients thoroughly; form into patties or links. Refrigerate for at least two hours to allow spices to blend. (Healthier Sausages)

Swedish Potato Sausage (Potatiskorv)

1 pound ground beef

½ pound ground pork

½ pound side pork (optional)

5 medium to large potatoes

1 large onion, chopped coarsely

½ teaspoon ground white pepper

½ teaspoon black pepper

1 ½ teaspoons salt

¼ teaspoon ground allspice

¼ teaspoon ground nutmeg

½ teaspoon garlic powder

Grind the meats and side pork separately through the course disk of grinder. Peel and boil the potatoes in lightly salted water for 10 minutes. Allow to cool. Cube the potatoes and mix together with chopped onion. Put this mixture through grinder. Add the ground meats to the potato/onion mixture. Add all remaining ingredients and mix well. Stuff the mixture into 4 to 5 inch links. Do not cut links apart at this time, tie ends together.

Swedish Potato Sausage (Potatiskorv - continued)

Put sausages into a heavy kettle; add one can chicken broth and enough water to cover sausages. Cover pot and simmer gently for 1 hour. Drain and refrigerate or freeze. (Home Sausage Making)

Scandinavian Sausage

1 ½ pounds pork

1/3 pound side pork

2 teaspoons allspice

½ teaspoon ginger

2 medium potatoes boiled and mashed or 1/6 cup of cornstarch

½ cup beef stock

1 teaspoon salt

1 teaspoon pepper

Grind meats finely, add remaining ingredients and stuff into casings.

United States

Kentucky-Style Pork Sausage

1 pound pork butt

½ pound side pork

1½ teaspoons salt

1 teaspoon black pepper

1 teaspoon sage

½ teaspoon cayenne

½ teaspoon coriander

¼ teaspoon nutmeg

¼ cup cold water

Grind pork and mix all ingredients together, stuff into casings. (The Complete Sausage Cookbook)

Tennessee Sausages

½ pound side pork and 1 ¾ pounds pork

1/8 teaspoon sage

1 tablespoon red pepper

1 ½ teaspoons salt and black pepper

½ teaspoon mace

1/8 teaspoon thyme

½ teaspoon garlic powder

½ teaspoon allspice

Grind, mix all ingredients, and form into patties or links. (The Complete Sausage Cookbook)

Southwestern Sausage Mixture

1 pound pork

¼ cup chopped onion

1 teaspoon garlic powder

2 to 3 chili peppers, chopped

1 teaspoon chili powder

1 teaspoon salt

½ teaspoon pepper

½ teaspoon cumin

½ teaspoon coriander

¼ cup vinegar

½ teaspoon Tabasco

Grind pork and onions, combine all ingredients. Form into patties of links. (The Complete Sausage Cookbook)

Ozark Sausage

1 pound pork

½ teaspoon salt

¼ teaspoon sage

½ teaspoon pepper

1 teaspoon red pepper

1 teaspoon brown sugar

Grind; mix all ingredients and form patties or links. (The Complete Sausage Cookbook)

Cajun Sausage

1 pound ground pork

¼ cup onion chopped fine

¼ teaspoon garlic powder

1¼ teaspoons salt

½ teaspoon pepper

½ teaspoon dried crushed red pepper

1/8 teaspoon paprika

1/8 teaspoon red pepper

½ teaspoon parsley flakes

¼ teaspoon allspice

Mix all ingredients thoroughly; form into patties or links. Refrigerate for at least two hours. (Healthier Sausages)

Fresh Country Brats

1 ½ pounds pork

1 pound veal or turkey

½ or ¼ pound side pork

1 tablespoon salt

1 teaspoon pepper

1 teaspoon sugar

1 teaspoon mace

1 teaspoon ground caraway seed

½ teaspoon ground ginger

½ cup milk

Grind meats, add remaining ingredients. Mix well and stuff into casings or form patties.

(The Complete Sausage Cookbook)

Chaurice New Orleans

2 pounds pork

1 pound side pork

1 large onion

1 teaspoon garlic powder

1½ teaspoons salt

2 sprigs parsley, minced

¼ teaspoon allspice

½ teaspoon hot chili pepper

½ teaspoon cayenne

½ teaspoon red pepper

1 teaspoon black pepper

1 teaspoon thyme

1 bay leaf, crushed

Grind meat, add remaining ingredients and mix well. Fill casings or form into patties.

(The Complete Sausage Cookbook)

Liver Sausage

1 ½ pounds pork shoulder

½ pound pork liver

1 ½ cups breadcrumbs

1 finely chopped onion

1 tablespoon salt

¼ teaspoon pepper

½ teaspoon dried thyme

½ teaspoon marjoram

Cover pork shoulder with water and boil until meat is soft. Reserve this liquid. Deeply score liver with a knife, cover pork liver with water and cook for 15 minutes, and throw out this liquid. Add the remaining ingredients, plus enough of the reserved liquid to make a soft mixture. Stuff into casings. Cook sausages in remaining pork liquid plus enough water to cover until sausages float for 10 to 20 minutes. After cooking, cool in cold water and hang to dry.

Liver Sausage #2

½ pound pork liver

¾ pound side pork

4 cups water

4 slices day old bread

½ cup chopped onion

2 tablespoons butter

1 teaspoon salt

½ teaspoon pepper

¼ teaspoon marjoram

Cook liver and side pork in water. Save broth. Put cooked meat in grinder. Cube bread then mix with meat. Pour hot broth over mixture until moist. Let stand. Sauté onions in butter. Put in meat mixture with remaining ingredients and mix well. Stuff into casings. Cook sausages in remaining liquid plus enough water to cover until sausages float, which requires 10 to 20 minutes. After cooking, cool in ice water and hang to dry. (St. Joseph Church Cookbook)

Cepvapcicci – Yugoslavian

2 pounds beef or 1 pound beef plus 1 pound veal

1 teaspoon garlic powder or to desired taste

1/3 cup warm water

1 ½ teaspoons sweet paprika

½ teaspoon cayenne

2 heaping tablespoons parsley

salt and pepper to taste

Cube meat and grind twice. Add garlic and water to meat and mix well. Add remaining ingredients and refrigerate for 1 hour. With wet hands shape the meat into sausages about three inches long and one inch thick. Grill over charcoal or broil. (Home Sausage Making)

Smoked Sausages

Bologna

3 pounds beef

2 pounds pork

½ pound pork fat or side pork

3 to 5 tablespoons salt

1 tablespoon pepper

1 teaspoon coriander

½ teaspoon mace

8 oz cold water

Grind meat using coarse grinder. Put in bowl, sprinkle with salt and seasonings, mix well and regrind. Add water and mix well, until mixture becomes sticky. Stuff tightly into beef casings. Hang in a cool place overnight, then smoke for 3 hours in well-ventilated smoker at 110 to 120 degrees. Put hot, smoked sausages in water heated to 160 to 175 degrees and let simmer 30 minutes, until sausage squeaks when pressed and released. Plunge into cold water to chill, hang to drip-dry. Refrigerate or freeze.

Milwaukee Frankfurters

5 pounds pork

3 ½ pounds side pork

1 ½ pounds beef

1 ½ pounds veal

4 pounds ice

5 oz salt

2 oz corn syrup

1 oz sugar

½ oz white pepper

¼ oz monosodium glutamate

1/8 oz nutmeg

1/8 oz ginger

1 teaspoon sodium nitrate

Chop beef, veal and pork combine with ice, salt, and sodium nitrite too a smooth paste. Mix together with spices in mixer for 5 to 6 minutes. Stuff into size 25 cellulose casings at 4-inch intervals and put in smoker.

Milwaukee Frankfurters - continued

Heat in smoker should be at 120 degree for 30 minutes, raise temperature to 140 degrees for 30 minutes and then to 160 to 165 degrees until an internal temperature of 160 degrees is reached. Cold shower for 5 minutes. Allow surface to dry and refrigerate or freeze.

(The Complete Sausage Cookbook)

Braunschweiger

1 ¼ pounds pork liver, trimmed and cubed

1 ¼ pounds pork butt, cubed

¼ cup ice water

1/8 cup nonfat dry milk

1 ½ tablespoons salt

1 ½ tablespoons sugar

1 tablespoon finely minced onion

½ teaspoon white pepper

½ teaspoon crushed mustard seed

¼ teaspoon marjoram

1/8 teaspoon allspice

1/8 teaspoon ascorbic acid or ¼ teaspoon saltpeter

Braunschweiger - continued

Grind the liver and pork separately and then mix thoroughly. Add the remaining ingredients, mix well and chill in freezer for 30 minutes and then regrind. Stuff into casings. Simmer in a large kettle of water for 1 hour or until internal temperature reaches 160 degrees. Remove from water, dry sausage and smoke for 2 hours at 160 degrees. After smoking place sausages in cold water for 30 minutes, remove and store.

(The Complete Sausage Cookbook)

Knackwurst Smoked – Bulgaria

2 ½ pounds pork

1 ½ pounds beef

½ pound side pork

3 tablespoons salt

5 cloves of garlic, crushed

1 ½ teaspoons cumin

¼ teaspoon salt tender

Grind meat; add all ingredients, mix and stuff. Allow to dry 24 hours in refrigerator. Smoke for 4 hours at 160 degrees. Cook in boiling water for 20 minutes before serving. (The Complete Sausage Cookbook)

Smoked Country Style Sausage

1 ½ pounds pork cubed or ground pork

1 pound beef or ground beef

½ cup water

1 ½ tablespoons salt

½ sugar

½ paprika

1 tablespoon white pepper

1 teaspoon ground mustard seed

1/8 teaspoon ascorbic acid

Grind the pork and beef fine. Mix meats and remaining ingredients. Stuff meat mixture into 3 to 4 inch links. Smoke until internal temperature reaches 160 degrees F. Simmer in 190 degree F. water for 30 minutes. Remove from kettle, place in cold water until internal temperature reaches 90 degrees, dry sausage, and refrigerate or freeze.

Summer Sausage

2 feet beef casing

2 pounds beef chuck

1 ½ pounds ground pork

2 tablespoons salt

½ tablespoon sugar

1/3 tablespoon white pepper

½ teaspoon crushed coriander seed

1 teaspoon whole black peppercorns

1/8 teaspoon nutmeg

½ cup water

1/8-teaspoon ascorbic acid (prevents discoloration)

Grind the beef through the fine blade twice. Grind the pork once and mix with beef. Prepare the casings. Stuff the meat into the casings and tie off into 6 to 8 inch lengths. Place in smoker until an internal temperature of 160-degree F. is reached. Cool in water and dry off. Let the sausage in the refrigerator for at least 2 days before eating. (Home Sausage Making)

Venison Sausages

Venison refers to the meat of moose, elk, reindeer, and white tail deer. Venison comes from wild game, pre-freeze meat before making sausage.

Venison may be used in any of the recipes in this book. For every pound of venison add 1/3 to ½ pound of ground pork or ¼ pound of side pork.

Smoking Instructions

Let sausage dry at room temperature for about 45 minutes after stuffing. Remove to smoker, which has been preheated to 120 degrees F. and leave dampers wide open. Sausage will continue to dry for about 45 minutes. After this period, gradually adjust smoker to 160/170 degrees F. allow sausage to smoke until the internal temperature reaches 160 degrees F.

Hot Venison Sausage Links

2 ½ pounds ground venison

1 pound beef suet, pork fat or side pork

2 tablespoons salt

1 tablespoon black pepper

1 teaspoon red or cayenne pepper

½ teaspoon sage

1 teaspoon paprika

Put venison and fat in pan. Spread all ingredients over meat, and mix thoroughly. Put through coarse grinder and then fine grinder plate. Be sure to keep meat cold, or mix in some ice cubes. Water is often necessary to make a suitable stuffing consistency. Stuff into sheep casing or make patties.

Smoked Venison Sausage

Marinade

½ cup red wine vinegar
1 teaspoon salt
½ onion sliced
¼ cup sliced carrots
1 clove of garlic, minced
1 bay leaf
Refrigerate marinated venison meat for 24 hours.

Smoked Venison Sausage

2 ½ pounds of venison

1 pound of pork, cubed

½ pound of side pork (venison is a very lean meat and needs some fat)

2 tablespoons salt

½ tablespoon thyme

1 tablespoon sugar

½ tablespoon black pepper

1 teaspoon pepper

1 teaspoon garlic powder

½ tablespoon paprika

½ tablespoon cayenne red pepper

1 cup water

½ teaspoon ascorbic acid

Smoked Venison Sausage - continued

Thaw venison, prepare marinate, pour over meat and refrigerate for 24 hours. Drain venison, discard marinate and grind meat. Grind pork and fat,mix with venison. Add remaining ingredients and mix thoroughly. Place sausage in refrigerator overnight. Prepare casings. Stuff the mixture into casings; tie off into 6 to 8 inch links. Smoke the sausage until an internal temperature of 160-degree F. is reached. Refrigerate or freeze.

Fresh Venison Sausage

3 pounds ground venison

1 pound ground pork

4 slices ground bacon

2 teaspoons onions, minced

1 teaspoon salt

¼ teaspoon black pepper

Mix all ingredients together in bowl and make into patties or links.

Venison Bologna

5 pounds ground venison

1 2/3 pounds ground pork or side pork

5 tablespoons salt

2 ½ tablespoons pepper

2 teaspoons coriander

1 teaspoon mace

10 oz water

Grind meats, add remaining ingredients except water and mix well. Regrind, add water and mix well. Stuff tightly in casings. Hang in refrigerator over night to dry. Put in a well-ventilated smoker for three hours at 120 to 130 degrees. Then put smoked sausages in water heated to 160 to 175 degrees and let simmer for at least 45 minutes or until sausage squeaks when pressed and released. Plunge in cold water to chill, hang in refrigerator to dry for 1-2 days before eating.

Venison Brats

2 ½ pounds venison

¾ pound side pork or ground pork

1 tablespoon salt

2 teaspoons pepper

1 ½ teaspoons sugar

1 teaspoon mace

1 teaspoon ground caraway seed

½ teaspoon ground ginger

1 teaspoon onion powder

1 teaspoon parsley

½ cup water

Grind, mix meat and add remaining ingredients. Mix well and stuff into casings or form patties.

Venison Italian Sausage

1 ½ pounds venison

2/3 pound ground pork

1 teaspoon paprika

1 teaspoon garlic powder

1 teaspoon fennel seed

1 teaspoon black pepper

¼ teaspoon crushed red pepper

¼ teaspoon red pepper flakes

1 teaspoon salt

1/2 teaspoon dried minced onion

Grind meat, add remaining ingredients, form into patties, stuff into casings or fry loose for pizza.

Venison Breakfast Sausage

1 ½ pounds venison

½ pound side pork

¾ cup chopped onion

¼ teaspoon garlic powder

1 ½ teaspoons parsley

1/8 teaspoon marjoram

¼ teaspoon cayenne pepper

1/8 teaspoon thyme

1/8 teaspoon sage

1/8 teaspoon basil

1 teaspoon black pepper

1 teaspoon salt

Grind meats, add remaining ingredients, form into patties or stuff into links.

Venison Wurst

1 ½ pounds venison

2/3 pound smoked bacon

½ cup chopped onion

½ cup milk

1 egg

¼ teaspoon ground cloves

1 teaspoon pepper

1 teaspoon chopped parsley

1 teaspoon salt

½ teaspoon nutmeg

½ teaspoon sage

Grind meats, add remaining ingredients, mix well. Stuff into casings—simmer for 30 minutes in water or chicken broth and then brown.

Venison Spanish Sausage

1 1/4 pounds venison

½ pound ground pork

2 tablespoons vinegar

½ teaspoon oregano

½ teaspoon garlic powder

½ teaspoon chili powder

1 teaspoon salt

¼ teaspoon ground cumin

¼ teaspoon crushed red pepper

¼ teaspoon cayenne pepper

Mix all ingredients thoroughly, form into patties or links. Refrigerate for at least two hours to allow spices to blend.

Venison Summer Sausage

1 ½ pounds venison

½ pound side pork

½ teaspoon onion powder

¼ teaspoon garlic powder

½ teaspoon liquid smoke

1 ¼ cups water

¾ teaspoon mustard seed

½ teaspoon black pepper

½ teaspoon salt

Grind meats, add remaining ingredients and mix well. Wrap in plastic wrap and refrigerate for 24 hours. Unwrap, bake on a rack in a pan with water at 300 degrees until internal temperature of sausages reaches 165 degrees. Put a pan on bottom of rack to catch drippings.

Bulk Venison

2 ½ pounds ground venison

1 pound beef suet, or pork fat or bacon

2 tablespoons salt

2 teaspoons black pepper

1 teaspoon red pepper or cayenne pepper

1 tablespoon sage

½ teaspoon saltpeter

2 tablespoons molasses

½ cup water

Grind venison through coarse cutter plate, then medium plate, spread out in pan and sprinkle with seasonings. Grind fat and add to venison mixture. Mix molasses with water, add to meat and mix well.

Miscellaneous Sausages

Head Cheese — Cure meat for 3-5 days in brine made with:

½ gallon water

6 oz salt

2 ½ oz sugar

1 oz Prague Powder/Instra Cure No 1

After curing, place meat loosely in kettle. Cover with sufficient water; cook approximately 1 ½ to 2 hours or until tender. After cooking, remove and cool. Grind meat; add remaining ingredients and sufficient amount of cooking stock to make a moist consistency. If forming in molds, place molds in ice water for approximately 2 hours to assist in rapid chilling. After chilling remove from molds and refrigerate.

Head Cheese

2 ¼ pounds pork

1 ¼ oz salt

1 ¼ oz gelatin, dissolved in 1 pint of warm water

1 ½ teaspoons ground white pepper

¼ teaspoon ginger

1/8 teaspoon allspice

¼ teaspoon ground caraway seed

¾ teaspoon onion powder

1/3 teaspoon ground marjoram

¾ teaspoon ground cloves

(The Complete Sausage Cookbook)

Seaman's Sausage

1 pound fish

½ medium onion, minced

¼ teaspoon pepper

1/8 teaspoon celery salt

1 teaspoon Dijon mustard

1/8 teaspoon cayenne pepper

10 single saltine crackers

¼ teaspoon salt

½ teaspoon poultry seasonings

1/8 teaspoon garlic powder

1 ½ teaspoons lemon juice

Use boneless, skinless fish scraps or fillets. Grind fine in food processor, add onion, crackers and blend well. Place mixture in bowl and add remaining Ingredients, blend with hands until thoroughly combined. Form into patties and fry in butter or bacon grease over medium heat until brown.

Meat-Oatmeal Sausage

2 ½ pounds ground pork

¾ pound turkey

6 slices of side pork

2 ½ cups oatmeal

1 tablespoon caraway seed

½ teaspoon mace

½ teaspoon allspice

1/8 teaspoon ginger

1 ½ tablespoons salt

½ teaspoon pepper.

Grind the meats and mix together. Add remaining ingredients and blend well. Stuff into casings, to cook boil a few minutes in water, then fry until browned.

Pork-Soy Bean Sausage

2 cups dried soybeans

1 pound smoked bacon

½ teaspoon ginger

½ teaspoon allspice

1 ½ teaspoons salt

½ teaspoon pepper

Place soy beans in water. Cover, bring to a boil and boil for 8-10 minutes and drain. Grind soybeans and cool. Grind meat, add soy beans, add spices and blend well. Stuff into casings, boil or fry.

Recipes Utilizing Sausages

Appetizers

Liver-Sausage Pate

½ pound bulk pork sausage

½ pound chicken livers

1 small onion

1/3 cup milk

1 tablespoon mustard

1 8 oz block cream cheese

1/8 teaspoon garlic powder

Cook sausage, onion until tender. Remove and sauté livers. In blender combine livers, milk and mustard, cover and blend well. Add sausage mixture, cream cheese and garlic powder, blend until smooth. Line a mold with plastic wrap, spoon mixture into mold and chill. Remove from mold when ready to serve. This pate is very easy to spread directly from the refrigerator.

Quick and Easy Liver Pate

8 oz liver sausage

1 8 oz block of cream cheese

1 teaspoon onion flakes

Blend together and chill.

Braunschweiger Spread

8 oz French onion chip dip

8 oz braunschweiger

Mix together, spread on crackers.

Braunschweiger Spread

8 oz braunschweiger

3 oz cream cheese

2 tablespoons pickle relish

1 tablespoon chopped onion

¼ teaspoon garlic powder.

Combine ingredients, blend well and chill.

Party Pizza

1 medium onion, chopped

1 pound Italian sausage

1 small can pizza sauce

16 oz Mozzarella

1 green pepper chopped

1 can black olives – optional

1 loaf French bread

Sauté Italian sausage and drain. Slice French bread in half lengthwise. Spread pizza sauce on each half. Layer remaining ingredients. Bake at 400 degrees until golden brown. Slice in 2 to 4 inch slices. May be frozen and reheated at 400 degrees for 10 minutes.

Pizza Appetizer

1 pound Italian sausage, browned and drained

1 pound Velveeta, cubed in small pieces

½ teaspoon garlic powder

½ teaspoon oregano

1 small can pizza sauce

1 loaf party rye

Mix together ingredients, but do not heat. Spread on rye bread. Freeze on cookie sheet. When frozen store in container until ready to use. Bake at 350 degrees until golden brown.

Italian Sloppy Joe

1 pound Italian sausage

1 packet Sloppy Joe mix

1 cup Mozzarella cheese

½ cup green pepper, chopped

½ cup onion, chopped

Brown sausage and add Sloppy Joe mix as directed. Fill buns with sausage mixture. Allow guest to add cheese, green peppers and onions as desired.

Drunk N' Dogs

1 cup brown sugar

1 cup whiskey or brandy

1 cup catsup

1 pound hot dogs, sliced into 1 inch pieces

Put all together and bring to a boil. Simmer for 15 minutes. Keep warm in a fondue pot.

(St. Joseph's Church Cookbook, Champion)

Delicious Stuffed Mushrooms

2 pounds large fresh mushrooms

½ cup bread crumbs, moistened with milk

½ pound pork sausage, browned and drained

2 tablespoons finely chopped onion

½ teaspoon Worcestershire sauce

½ teaspoon seasoned salt

Clean, dry, remove stems from mushroom crowns. Combine other ingredients; fill center of each crown. Place on cookie sheet and brush with melted butter. Broil 5-8 minutes until hot and lightly browned. Variation: May top with Mozzarella cheese or Swiss cheese before broiling.

BREAKFAST/BRUNCH

Breakfast Burritos

½ pound breakfast sausage

2 tablespoons chopped onion

1 small can (4-oz) mushrooms

4 eggs

¾ cup Veletta cheese

4 flour tortillas

Brown sausage and drain drippings. Add onions, and mushrooms sauté until tender. Beat eggs slightly, cook with onions and mushrooms. Place sausage on tortilla, egg mixture and 2 tablespoons of cheese. Fold up tortilla. 3 servings

Breakfast Pizza

1 can crescent rolls

2/3 pound breakfast sausage

8 oz can sliced mushrooms

½ cup milk

6 eggs

½ cup chopped onions

¼ cup chopped green peppers

½ teaspoon oregano

Pat dough in buttered 9x13 pan. Brown sausage, drain and place in pan. Sprinkle with cheese and mushrooms. Beat the eggs and combine with milk, oregano, onions, green peppers, salt and pepper to taste. Pour over the other ingredients. Bake at 425 degrees F. for 30 minutes. (St. Joseph's Church Cookbook)

Cheese and Sausage Quiche

1 unbaked 9 inch pie shell

1 cup shredded cheddar cheese

1/3 pound pork sausage, cooked, drained and crumbled

1 4 oz can mushroom pieces, drained

2 eggs, slightly beaten

2 teaspoons flour

½ teaspoon salt

½ cup half and half

1 tablespoon butter, melted

Preheat oven to 400 degrees and bake pie shell for 8 to 10 minutes. Let cool. Reduce oven heat to 375 degrees. Layer the cheese, sausage and mushrooms in pie shell. Combine remaining ingredients, mix well until blended. Pour half the egg mixture into pie shell and bake for 45 minutes or until set. Let cool for 5 minutes and cut into wedges.

ENTREES

Spaghetti Sauce

1 ½ pounds Italian sausage

1 celery stalk, diced

1 medium onion, chopped

¼ cup dried onion

1 medium can tomato sauce

1 medium can tomato paste

½ teaspoon garlic salt

1/3 green pepper, chopped

¼ teaspoon oregano

¼ teaspoon basil

1 bay leave

Brown sausage and drain drippings. Add remaining ingredients and simmer for 30 to 45 minutes to thicken sauce.

Polenta With Sausage

1 pound Italian sausage

1 small onion

1 tablespoon olive oil

1 #2 can tomatoes

½ teaspoon salt and pepper

1 cup yellow corn meal

1 cup grated Parmesan cheese

Brown sausage and onion in oil. Add tomatoes and seasonings. Simmer for 1 hour, stirring occasionally. While sauce is cooking, prepare corn meal. Bring 1 ½ quarts salted water to a boil, pour corn meal into water, stirring constantly to prevent lumps. Cook uncovered over low heat until corn meal leaves sides of pan, about 30 minutes. Remove from heat and stir in ½ cup Parmesan cheese. Pour half the corn meal on a large platter. Pour ½ the sauce over corn meal, sprinkle with remaining cheese. Repeat layers and serve immediately. Serves 4 (St. Joseph Church Cookbook, DePere)

One Dish Meal

½ pound metwurst or pork sausage

1 cup sauerkraut

2 cups mashed potatoes

Cut metwurst in 2-inch pieces and cook slowly. Drain sauerkraut and rinse. Potatoes should be mashed and seasoned. Put meat in casserole, sauerkraut and then mashed potatoes. Bake at 375 degrees oven for 30 minutes.

Polish Sausages and Sauerkraut

1 can (1-lb) sauerkraut

2 long Polish sausages

½ teaspoon caraway seeds

2 tablespoons sugar

2 tablespoon chopped onion

2 cups water

Put all ingredients into saucepan and simmer for 1 hour.

Brats in Beer

1 pound brats

12 oz beer

1/8 lb butter

1 medium onion sliced

¼ teaspoon salt and pepper

Brown brats either on stove or grill. Melt butter in 2-quart saucepan. Add beer, onion, salt and pepper. Bring to boil. Add brats and simmer for 1 ½ to 2 hours.

Wild Rice and Sausage Stuffing

¼ cup finely chopped onions

1 4 oz can mushrooms

1 6 oz box Uncle Ben's Long/Wild Rice

¼ cup butter

½ pound pork sausage

1 teaspoon salt

1 teaspoon pepper

1 egg

Sauté onions and mushrooms in butter, remove from pan. Fry sausage until lightly brown, remove from heat and drain grease. Cook rice according to package directions. Combine all ingredients and add egg to bind mixture. Bake at 350 degrees for 1 hour.

Delicious Lasagna

4 oz lasagna noodles

1 8 oz block cream cheese

½ cup sour cream

2 oz Mozzarella cheese

1/8 cup chopped parsley

1 cup spaghetti sauce

Cook noodles, drain. Mix cottage cheese, sour cream, Mozzarella cheese and parsley. Place ½ of noodles in 9x13 pan. Put half of cheese mixture on top. Put a layer of sauce. Repeat with noodles, cheese and sauce. Cover and bake at 350 degrees for 60 to 70 minutes. Let stand 15 minutes before serving.

Quick Sauce: 1 pound Italian sausage, 1 cup tomato sauce, 1 can 6 oz tomato paste, 1 teaspoon garlic powder, ½ teaspoon oregano and ½ cup chopped onion. Brown meat and drain. Add remaining ingredients and simmer for 10 minutes.

Sausage Skillet Supper

½ pound pork sausage

1 can tomato soup

1 small can kidney beans, rinsed and drained

1 cup cooked rice

1 cup water

1/3 cup salsa

Brown sausage and drained. Add remaining ingredients. Bring to boil and simmer for 30 minutes or until rice is tender.

Sausage and Rice

1 /2 pound pork sausage

1 celery stalks, diced

¼ onion, chopped finely

1 pkg. dry chicken-noodle soup

1/3 cup raw instant rice

1 ½ cup water

Brown sausage, onions and drain. Mix all ingredients together and place in a greased casserole dish. Bake uncovered for 45 minutes to 1 hour at 350 degrees.

Easy Sausage Casserole

1-cup spaghetti sauce previously mentioned or 1 small jar of spaghetti sauce and brown ½ pound Italian sausage.

8 oz of cooked noodles

½ cup grated Parmesan cheese

½ cup shredded Mozzarella cheese

1 small can mushrooms

Combine all ingredients except ¼ cup Mozzarella in casserole dish. Sprinkle remaining Mozzarella cheese on top. Bake for 30 minutes at 350 degrees.

Baked Beans-Chili Style

1 pkg. small wieners or slice 4 wieners into 1 inch pieces

¼ cup chopped onions

1 can 16 oz Pork and Beans

½ cup chili sauce

1/3 cup brown sugar

Cook onions until tender. Combine all remaining ingredients. Spoon into casserole dish and bake for 45 minutes until bubbly.

Potato Sausage Casserole

½ pound pork sausage

1 can cream of potato soup

1/3 cup milk

½ cup chopped onion

½ teaspoon salt

½ teaspoon pepper

1 ½ cups hash brown potatoes

1 cup shredded cheddar cheese

Brown sausage and drain. Combine remaining ingredients and put in a greased casserole dish. Bake at 350 degrees for 45 minutes; uncover to brown lightly the top.

Kids Casserole

2 cups sliced potatoes

3 hot dogs sliced

2 tablespoons chopped onions

½ cup frozen corn

1 can cream of potato soup combined with ½ cup milk.

1 teaspoon mustard

½ teaspoon salt

½ teaspoon pepper

In a greased casserole dish combine potatoes, hot dogs, onions and corn. Combine soup, milk, mustard, salt and pepper. Pour over ingredients in casserole dish. Bake at 350 degrees for 1 hour or until potatoes are tender.

Italian Shepherd's Pie

1 pound Italian sausage

½ cup frozen corn

½ cup chopped onions

½ teaspoon salt

¼ teaspoon oregano

1 small can mushroom

½ cup shredded Cheddar cheese

½ cup Mozzarella cheese

½ cup Bisquick Original baking mix

1 cup milk

2 eggs

Brown sausage and onions, drain. Spread in the bottom of a greased casserole dish. Mix remaining ingredients and pour into casserole. Bake at 375 degrees until knife comes out clean.

SOUP

Sausage Chowder

½ pound fully cooked smoked sausage, thinly sliced

½ cup onion chopped

2 cups diced potatoes

1 cup diced carrots

½ cup chopped cabbage

2 cups beef or chicken broth

2 cups water

1 teaspoon dried parsley

½ teaspoon dried basil

½ teaspoon salt

1 small can whole kernel corn

1 (large can) cream-style corn

6 oz half and half

Sausage Chowder - continued

Brown sausage and onions. Add remaining ingredients except cream style corn and half-and-half. Simmer until potatoes and carrots are tender. Add cream style corn and half-and-half, cook for 5 to 10 minutes until heated through.

Hearty Italian Soup

½ pound mild Italian sausage

1/8 cup chopped green pepper

¼ cup chopped onion

1 16 oz can tomatoes, cup up, undrained

1 8 oz can tomato sauce

1 cup water

1 tablespoon chicken bouillon

½ teaspoon garlic powder

½ teaspoon oregano

½ cup small shell macaroni

Shredded Mozzarella, Cheddar or American cheese

Brown sausage, green pepper and onion drain. Add remaining ingredients except macaroni and cheese. Cover and simmer for 30 minutes. Stir in macaroni and simmer an additional 30 minutes or until macaroni is tender. Top each serving with cheese.

Minestrone

½ pound Italian sausage, browned and drained

½ cup onion, diced

1 teaspoon garlic powder

1 small jar thick spaghetti sauce

1 cups water

1 tablespoon beef broth

½ cup carrots, diced

½ cup celery, sliced

1 teaspoon salt

1 tablespoon parsley

1 small can kidney beans

½ cup small macaroni shells

2 tablespoons grated cheese

Put all ingredients except last three ingredients in kettle. Simmer for 30 minutes. Add kidney beans and shells, simmer for 20 minutes longer or until shells are tender. Serve with cheese sprinkled on top.

Sauerkraut Soup

2 cups water

2 medium potatoes, diced

½ teaspoon salt

½ cup onion, chopped

1 tablespoon flour

½ pound Polish sausage, sliced into small pieces

½ cup sour cream

¼ teaspoon garlic powder

½ teaspoon dill weed

½ teaspoon pepper

1 small can sauerkraut

In kettle bring water, potatoes, salt and onion to boil. Cook until potatoes are tender. Add sausage, sauerkraut (undrained), garlic powder, pepper and dill weed. Simmer for 15 minutes. Blend sour cream and flour, stir about 1 cup of hot mixture into sour cream. Add slowly to soup mixture, blending well. Heat thoroughly but not boiling.

CONVERSION CHART FOR MEASUREMENTS

Abbreviations Commonly Used:

Tsp. – teaspoon	oz – ounce or ounces
Tbs. – tablespoon	lb. – pound or pounds
C – cup	min. – minute or minutes
Pt – pint	hr – hour or hours
Qt – quart	mod – moderate or moderately

Simplified Measurements

60 drops = 1 teaspoon
dash = less than 1/8 teaspoon
3 teaspoons = 1 tablespoon
2 tablespoons = 1/8 cup or 1 ounce
4 tablespoons = ¼ cup or 2 ounces
5 1/3 tablespoons = 1/3 cup
8 tablespoons = ½ cup = 4 ounces
10 2/3 tablespoons = 2/3 cup
12 tablespoons = ¾ cup = 6 ounces
14 tablespoons = 7/8 cup
16 tablespoons = 1 cup = 8 ounces
1 cup = 8 ounces = ½ pint
2 cups = 16 ounces = 1 pint
4 cups = 32 ounces/1 quart
8 cups = 64 ounces = 4 pints = 2 quarts = ½ gallon
16 cups = 128 ounces = 8 pints = 4 quarts = 1 gallon

References

Hawkins, Nancy and Arthur. 1976 The American Regional Cookbook. Prenctice Hall Inc.

McIntosh, E. 1996 American Food Habits. Praegers Publishing.

Kutas, Rytek. Great Sausage Recipes and Meat Curing. The Sausage Maker, Inc.

Depeau-Gilson, Judy. 1996. Healthier Sausages. Judy's Kitchen.

Reavis, C. 1948. Home Sausage Making. Garden Ways Inc.

Sleight, Jack. 1995 The Complete Sausage Cookbook. Stackpole Books.

Riddle, P., M.J. Danley. 1977 The Complete Sausage Cookbook. San Francisco Book Company, Inc. 9

Kitchen Klassics (St. Joseph Church, DePere) 2nd printing 1971, DePere Wi.

A Collection of Recipes (St. Joseph Church, Champion) 1978, Fundcraft Publishing Inc.

About the Author

As long as I can remember, food preparation has been an enjoyable experience. I can never pass up a cookbook of magazine containing recipes without examining the contents. The adventure of creating a mouth watering meal is a challenging and rewarding experience.

Printed in the United Kingdom
by Lightning Source UK Ltd.
107615UKS00003B/301